GETTING TO KNOW
THE U.S. PRESIDENTS

WOODROW
WILSON

TWENTY-EIGHTH PRESIDENT
1913 – 1921

WRITTEN AND ILLUSTRATED BY MIKE VENEZIA

CHILDREN'S PRESS®
A DIVISION OF SCHOLASTIC INC.
NEW YORK   TORONTO   LONDON   AUCKLAND   SYDNEY
MEXICO CITY   NEW DELHI   HONG KONG
DANBURY, CONNECTICUT

Reading Consultant: Nanci R. Vargus, Ed.D., Assistant Professor, School of Education, University of Indianapolis

Historical Consultant: Marc J. Selverstone, Ph.D., Assistant Professor, Miller Center of Public Affairs, University of Virginia

Photographs © 2007: AP/Wide World Photos: 32; Brown Brothers: 16; Corbis Images: 19, 28, 31 (Bettmann), 6 (Medford Historical Society Collection), 30; Getty Images/MPI/Hulton Archive: 7; Punch Ltd., www.punch.co.uk: 21; Superstock, Inc./Culver Pictures: 3; The Art Archive/Picture Desk: 4 (Culver Pictures), 25 (Imperial War Museum), 26 (Eileen Tweedy), 27 (Laurie Platt Winfrey/Whitney Museum of American Art); The Image Works/Mary Evans Picture Library: 20, 24; U.S. Senate Collection, Center for Legislative Archives: 18; Woodrow Wilson Presidential Library: 10, 13.

Colorist for illustrations: Dave Ludwig

Library of Congress Cataloging-in-Publication Data

Venezia, Mike.
  Woodrow Wilson / written and illustrated by Mike Venezia.
     p. cm. — (Getting to know the U.S. presidents)
  ISBN-10: 0-516-22632-0 (lib. bdg.)   0-516-25462-6 (pbk.)
  ISBN-13: 978-0-516-22632-3 (lib. bdg.)   978-0-516-25462-3 (pbk.)
  1. Wilson, Woodrow, 1856-1924—Juvenile literature. 2. Presidents—United States—Biography—Juvenile literature. I. Title.
  E767.V29 2006
  973.91'3'092-dc22
                                                                                    2006000461

1 2 3 4 5 6 7 8 9 10 R 16 15 14 13 12 11 10 09 08 07

President Woodrow Wilson at his desk in the White House

Woodrow Wilson was the twenty-eighth president of the United States. He was born in the small town of Staunton, Virginia, in 1856. President Wilson was a strong leader with fresh ideas who knew exactly what he wanted to do.

Woodrow Wilson as president of Princeton University

Woodrow Wilson was the best-educated president ever. Before he became president, Woodrow was a lawyer, a college professor, president of Princeton University, and governor of New Jersey. Woodrow studied American history to learn what had worked well in the past and what had not. He spent years forming ideas about how to run the United States government just the right way.

Woodrow Wilson never forgot about the damage that was done to the South during the Civil War.

As a young boy, Woodrow used his first name, Thomas. Tommy Wilson was born just before the Civil War began. His family moved to Georgia when he was about a year old. While growing up, Tommy saw Union soldiers marching through his town. He never forgot the destruction that war brought.

During and after the war, there were hardly any schools in the South. Woodrow's father, who was a minister and a very good teacher, taught his children at home. Amazingly, Tommy started out having a hard time with his studies. He didn't learn the alphabet until he was nine, and he could hardly read until he was twelve years old. Today, some experts think Tommy Wilson may have had a learning disability such as dyslexia.

A childhood drawing by Tommy Wilson

Even though Tommy Wilson had a difficult time learning to read and write, he did well in other areas. Tommy loved discussing the many history books and stories his father

read to him. He often joined in on adult
conversations. Tommy seemed to understand
complicated world events, even at an early age.

In 1873, when Tommy was sixteen years old, he went off to Davidson College in North Carolina. He wasn't really ready to go away to school, though. After one year there, he returned home, homesick and in poor health. A year later, when he felt better, Tommy Wilson tried out the College of New Jersey, which today is called Princeton University.

Wilson (holding his hat at right) with a group of friends at Princeton

Tommy really liked Princeton. He made lots of friends there. He joined and started all kinds of clubs and organizations. Tommy Wilson became one of the best debaters and speakers the school had ever seen.

Most importantly, Tommy discovered he loved politics. He decided he would become a government leader someday. He also decided to start using his middle name.

After graduating from Princeton, Woodrow Wilson went to the University of Virginia to study law. He felt the best way to prepare for a political career was to become a lawyer. Even though Woodrow was totally bored studying law, he managed to pass his law exam. Woodrow and a classmate, Edward Renick, opened up a law office in Atlanta, Georgia.

Ellen Axson Wilson

Unfortunately, the two new lawyers hardly got any business at all. Woodrow wasn't too disappointed, though. He decided to try another career. Woodrow went back to school to become a college professor. He studied his favorite subjects, history and politics, at Johns Hopkins University.

It was during this time that he met his future wife, Ellen Axson. Ellen was very interested in history and politics, too. She was also a talented art student.

Woodrow Wilson ended up becoming a great college professor. He taught at Bryn Mawr College in Pennsylvania, and then Wesleyan University in Connecticut.

In 1890, Woodrow was happy to return to Princeton to teach government and politics. He became a superstar teacher there. He made difficult subjects fun and inspired his students to want to learn more. Students packed Professor Wilson's classes, and often stood up to clap and cheer at the end of his lectures. The people who ran Princeton liked Woodrow a lot, too. In 1902, they asked him to be president of the university. Woodrow did a great job. He helped make Princeton one of the best schools in the world.

People were impressed with Woodrow Wilson (center) when he was president of Princeton University.

Woodrow Wilson was getting attention all over the state of New Jersey for the remarkable job he was doing as Princeton's president. Then something happened that made his greatest dream come true. Woodrow was asked by members of the New Jersey Democratic Party to run for governor of the state. For years, there had been some dishonest politicians running New Jersey.

Most people in New Jersey wanted an honest governor who would fix things up. Woodrow promised he would be the man to do the job. In 1910, he was elected governor of New Jersey. Woodrow kept his promise. He found ways to get rid of shady politicians and pass laws to improve the lives of everyday working people.

A political cartoon showing the three-way presidential race between Teddy Roosevelt, Woodrow Wilson, and William H. Taft

Woodrow Wilson's reputation as an excellent governor spread all over the country. Soon, some Democratic leaders asked Woodrow to run for president of the United States. Woodrow agreed. His opponents in the election were President William H. Taft and former president Teddy Roosevelt.

When all the votes were counted, Woodrow had won. He became president in 1913. President Wilson got to work right away. He had a plan and explained it well to the American people. With the people's support, President Wilson got some important laws passed. These laws would especially help the nation's poorest working people.

President Wilson was known as a great speaker.

This political cartoon shows President Wilson as a hero who has arrived to regulate the nation's banking system, which had been run by a few wealthy bankers.

One of the first things President Wilson did was lower tariffs. Tariffs are taxes placed on products that come from foreign countries. He then helped set up a new banking system called the Federal Reserve. This system controlled money in the United States. It helped protect the economy when money problems came up.

A political cartoon showing President Wilson acting as a "referee" to control trusts

President Wilson continued to control giant companies called trusts. He made them keep their prices fair to give smaller businesses a better chance to compete. But just when it seemed like everything was going well, tragedy struck Woodrow Wilson.

On August 6, 1914, President Wilson's wife, Ellen, died. Woodrow Wilson was so upset he could hardly go on. But the president had to go on, because another tragic event happened right around the same time.
A war broke out in Europe.

The war included England, France, and Russia on one side, and Germany, Austria-Hungary, and Turkey on the other. President Wilson did everything he could to keep the United States out of the war. He sent a peace mission to Europe to see if things could be worked out peacefully. But no one there was interested at all.

LEST WE FORGET

FAC-SIMILE OF MEDAL STRUCK BY GERMANY
TO COMMEMORATE THE EVENT
Translation of wording on Medal
BUSINESS ABOVE EVERYTHING   NO CONTRABAND — THE

The Sinking of the Lusitania.
May 7th 1915.

The sinking of the *Lusitania* was one event that led to U.S. involvement in World War I.

In 1915, President Wilson met and fell in love with a woman named Edith Galt. After dating for a short time, the couple decided to get married. Edith came along at just the right time. Woodrow really needed her support as the world headed toward war. As hard as he tried, President Wilson couldn't keep the United States out of the war. Germany kept using its submarines to sink passenger and cargo ships.

When the British passenger liner *Lusitania* was torpedoed, 128 American passengers lost their lives. Finally, in 1917, after German submarines sank several American cargo ships, President Wilson asked Congress to declare war on Germany.

World War I turned out to be more horrible than anyone expected. It was the first time modern weapons were used. Machine guns, airplanes, and worst of all, poison gas, caused millions of lives to be lost.

This painting by John Singer Sargent shows soldiers affected by poison gas during World War I (Imperial War Museum, London)

This famous World War I poster shows Uncle Sam asking Americans to volunteer to fight in the war.

I WANT YOU
FOR U.S. ARMY
NEAREST RECRUITING STATION

As soon as Congress declared war, thousands of men joined or were drafted into the army. The United States fought in the war for a little over a year. When American soldiers arrived in Europe, they quickly helped England, France, Italy, and their allies defeat Germany. By November 11, 1918, the war was over.

Even before the fighting ended, President Wilson had worked out a peace plan. The

This painting by George Luks shows people celebrating the end of World War I in 1918 (Whitney Museum of American Art, New York)

president wanted all enemy nations to be dealt with fairly. He had many more ideas for peace, too. He felt the most important one, though, was to form a League of Nations. President Wilson wanted countries of the world to join together so they could discuss their problems before arguments turned to war.

During peace talks in France, President Wilson presented his plan. Some nations disagreed with him. They didn't want to treat their enemies fairly, and especially wanted to punish Germany.

President Wilson returned to the United States disappointed that some changes had been made to his original plan. He was happy, however, that the European nations had agreed to keep his favorite part, the League of

President Wilson (far right) and other world leaders at the 1919 Paris Peace Conference

Nations. Now, all the president had to do was to get the U.S. Senate to approve it.

Unfortunately, the Senate didn't approve it. Some jealous senators who had been left out of the peace talks worked against Woodrow Wilson's peace treaty. Other members of Congress didn't want the United States getting involved in the problems of foreign nations, even if it meant preventing war.

President Wilson during his cross-country trip to promote the League of Nations

President Wilson tried so hard to get the American people and Congress to accept his plan that he made himself ill. After traveling around the country giving speeches to promote the League, Woodrow began to feel terrible and had to be rushed home.

This political cartoon shows President Wilson trying to "sell" the League of Nations, shown here as a horse, to the U.S. Senate.

As soon as he returned to the White House, President Wilson had a stroke that left him half paralyzed. The president was now too sick and worn down to fight for his peace plan. Even though some European countries joined the League of Nations, the United States never did. Still, President Wilson won the 1919 Nobel Peace Prize for his efforts to promote world peace.

Woodrow Wilson and his second wife, Edith, toward the end of Wilson's presidency

For the last seventeen months of his second term, President Wilson could hardly work. His wife, Edith, took over many of his responsibilities. Some people even called Edith the first woman president.

Woodrow Wilson was an important president who not only got the United States through World War I, but supported many laws that made life safer and more fair for the people of the United States. After President Wilson's term ended in 1921, he and Edith retired to their home in Washington, D.C. Woodrow Wilson died peacefully at home in 1924.